First published in 2007 by
Ravette Publishing Ltd
Unit 3, Tristar Centre, Star Road,
Partridge Green, West Sussex RH13 8RA

(www.garfield.com)

ISBN: 978-1-84161-282-9

GET A GRIP!

RAVETTE PUBLISHING

GRIP IT AND RIP IT!

GIVE ME COFFEE AND NO ONE GETS HURT

The more things change,
the more I go insane.

I might as well exercise. I'm in a bad mood anyway.

have a
nice day!

ASSESS THE SITUATION CALMLY.

THEN PANIC!

Beneath this chaos
is a really big mess!

I'm an "evening" person in a "morning" world.

TAKE GOLF ONE TANTRUM AT A TIME.

IT'S BEEN
ONE OF THOSE DAYS
ALL WEEK.

GET
A
GRIP

"The party's not over until the fat cat burps"

I'd give up golf,
but I need the stress.

GO ON, TEMPT ME.

In a perfect world, oranges would have zips.

DON'T WORRY —
I'M ON TOP OF IT.

Other GARFIELD Gift Books published by Ravette ...

	ISBN	Pric
Gift Books (hardback)		
Don't Know Don't Care	978-1-84161-279-9	£4.9
I Don't Do Ordinary	978-1-84161-281-2	£4.9
Keep your attitude, I have my own	978-1-84161-278-2	£4.9
Little Books (paperback)		
C-c-c-caffeine	978-1-84161-183-9	£2.5
Food 'n' Fitness	978-1-84161-145-7	£2.5
Laughs	978-1-84161-146-4	£2.5
Love 'n' Stuff	978-1-84161-147-1	£2.5
Surf 'n' Sun	978-1-84161-186-0	£2.5
The Office	978-1-84161-184-6	£2.5
Zzzzzz	978-1-84161-185-3	£2.5

All Garfield books are available at your local bookshop or from the publisher at the address below.

Just send your order with your payment and name and address details to:-
Ravette Publishing, Unit 3, Tristar Centre, Star Road, Partridge Green,
West Sussex RH13 8RA (tel: 01403 711443   email: ravettepub@aol.com)

Prices and availability are subject to change without prior notice.

Please enclose a cheque or postal order made payable to Ravette Publishing
to the value of the cover price of the books and allow the following for UK p&p:-

70p for the first book + 40p for each additional book.